CW00505364

THE ART OF FLORISTRY

WIRING, MOUNTING AND ASSEMBLY TECHNIQUES

WEDDING FLOWERS

FLORISTRY BY JANE WESTON
PHOTOGRAPHY BY MARK WESTON

Published by
THE FOUR SEASONS PUBLISHING COMPANY (IRELAND) LTD
26, FITZWILLIAM SQUARE, DUBLIN, 2.

Main U.K. Distributors
FOUR SEASONS PUBLICATIONS,
THE STABLES, MONXTON, Nr. ANDOVER, HANTS, SP11 8AT.

© THE FOUR SEASONS PUBLISHING COMPANY (IRELAND) LTD

SBN 901131 07 5

OTHER TITLES AVAILABLE
in full colour

Spring Flower Arranging	*Church Flower Arranging*
Summer Flower Arranging	*Christmas Flower Arranging*
Autumn Flower Arranging	*Dried Flower Arranging*
Winter Flower Arranging	*Party Flower Arranging*
Wedding Flowers in Colour	*Gift and Sympathy Flowers in Colour*

in black and white

The Art of Floristry—Funeral Flowers	*In Remembrance*
Flowers for the Bride	*Profitable Window Display*

Contents

Preface

Floristry is not only the backbone of the world wide flower industry, but also an important factor in the profitable management of most flower shops.

The florist uses vast quantities of flowers every year in order to satisfy the public demand for artistic wedding flowers, floral arrangements and funeral tributes. It is surprising therefore, that until now no comprehensive instruction books have been available for helping new entrants to the flower industry to learn and master the art and skills involved.

It is because of this unfortunate gap that this book has been produced. It is one of a series of instruction books aimed at imparting essential information on the techniques of floristry, previously conveyed to the beginner solely by word of mouth and time-taking personal demonstration by skilled and trained florists.

This book, on Wedding Flowers, is divided into three sections. (1) Equipment required. (2) Wiring and Mounting Techniques. (3) Assembly Techniques. Although there are, no doubt, other satisfactory methods of creating wedding designs, the techniques which have been explained in detail are practical and efficient and are similar to those taught at a number of leading Flower Schools.

All the designs which are dealt with in the Assembly section come from *Flowers for the Bride* and *Wedding Flowers in Colour*—the two basic Design books which are in regular use by thousands of florists throughout the world as important sales aids.

The flower industry is constantly expanding as the general public become more sophisticated and increasingly appreciate beautiful flowers combined with skilful craftsmanship. Consequently there is a shortage of trained florists. New entrants and trainees may find, therefore, that they can master the basic techniques more quickly by studying this book and soon become able to participate competently in the wonderful world of floristry and flowers.

Mark Weston

Equipment required

All the items of equipment which are required for the make-up of wedding flowers are straightforward and easily obtainable. A few comments are called for, as follows:—

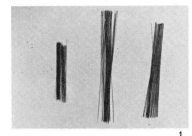

Wires
24° × 7″, 22° × 14″, 20° × 12″.

Satin Ribbons
1½″, 1″, 2″.

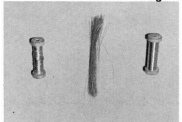

32° silver reel wire.
32° × 7″ silver rose wire.
36° silver reel wire.

WIRES

Wires are obtainable in several different gauges and lengths. The lower the gauge the thicker the wire, e.g. a 20° wire is thicker than a 24° wire.

Wires which are 24° or thinner are usually sold already cut to a 7″ length and are referred to, in the Trade, as "Rose Wires". They are normally silvered, which makes them cleaner and easier to handle.

Wires which are 22° or thicker come in a considerable number of different lengths and are usually referred to as "Stub Wires". It is not normally possible to obtain these Stub Wires silvered, owing to the additional cost of this process.

Both rose wires and stub wires, are sold by weight.

Reel wire is also available in various gauges, either silvered or black. It is best to specify "silvered" for wedding work.

1″ pins, guttapercha, "sellotape".

Needle and cotton, florists' scissors, water sprayer.

GUTTAPERCHA

This is a ½″ tape made of Latex, which is ideal for binding and covering wires, so as to present a neat and finished appearance. It is available in two shades of green, natural fawn colour and in white. White is mostly used for wedding work.

Bridesmaid's basket, sphagnum moss posy frill.

Hat elastic, tissue paper, oasis, wine glass.

Wiring and Mounting Techniques

All flowers, florets and leaves when used for wedding work, have to be either wired or mounted or both. There does not appear to be a precise definition for these two processes, so, after much consultation with leading florists, we have decided to give the following definitions in order to clarify the position.

WIRING
When a flower requires reinforcement of the natural stem with a wire in order either to strengthen the stem or to make it more flexible and capable of retaining a desired position, the process is called "Wiring".

MOUNTING
When it is necessary to substitute the natural stem of a flower with an artificial wire one, or when it is necessary to provide a floret or leaf with a wire stem, this process is called "Mounting". Sometimes a subject has to be mounted twice. Firstly on to a thin wire and then on to a thicker wire.

SIZE OF WIRES
Wires are obtainable in many different gauges and lengths, but we have only made use of four different sizes of cut wires and two different gauges of reel wire. This gives entirely satisfactory results in normal circumstances. It is desirable, however, to have other sizes of wire available to cope with the abnormal—such as the very weak stemmed flower which must have a slightly thinner wire than usual to cope with the situation.

GROUPS
In the following Section it will be noted that the various techniques are divided up into sixteen Groups, each distinguished by a different letter. At the end of each Group there is a list of other flowers which require similar treatment. These lists are obviously not exhaustive, but cover many of the subjects which are used in wedding work.

At first sight it may seem unnecessary to have so many Groups. For instance, the reason for separating the Rose from Zinnias and Gardenias may not be apparent. When you appreciate, however, that the Rose has a solid stem, the Zinnia a hollow one and the Gardenia stem is so woody that the mounting wire has to be pushed through the calyx instead, the reason why these three flowers have been grouped separately becomes evident.

Wiring and Mounting Techniques

Group A

Mounting a Rose
Mounting a Cymbidium Orchid

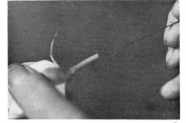

Mounting a Rose
Insert 22° × 14" wire into ¾" of Rose stalk and push wire up into base of Rose.

8

Wire inserted.

9

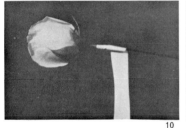
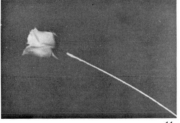
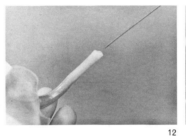
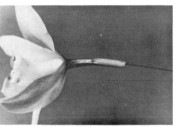

Wire being covered with gutta.

10

Mounting completed.

11

Mounting a Cymbidium Orchid
Insert 22° × 14" wire into the remaining 1" stem.

12

Push the wire into the base of the Orchid.

13

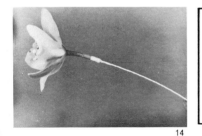

Guttaring completed.

14

Similar requirements for
A.Y.R. Spray Chrysanthemum, Gerbera, Hellebore, Tulip.

Group B

Mounting a single Zinnia

15

Insert 22° × 14" wire into ¾" of hollow stem and push into the base of flower.

16

Insert 32° × 7" Rose wire through the stem (about ¼" from flower base) avoiding previously inserted wire. 4" of Rose wire should project on one side and 3" on the other.

17

Bend Rose wire into a hairpin shape and wind 4" Rose wire leg around the bottom of the stalk and the 3" length of Rose wire (see 21).

18

Guttaring completed. (See 23, 24, 25.)

Similar requirements for
Cornflower, Daffodil, Eucharis Lily, Marguerite, Narcissus, Ranunculus.

Group C

Mounting a Stephanotis Floret
Mounting a Chincherincheree Floret
Point of insertion for a Freesia Floret and a Hyacinth Floret

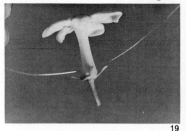

19

Mounting a Stephanotis floret
Insert a 32° × 7" Rose wire through base of flower having approximately 4" projecting on one side and 3" on the other.

20

Bend Rose wire to form a hairpin.

21

Wind 4" leg of Rose wire around the bottom part of the stalk and the other Rose wire leg.

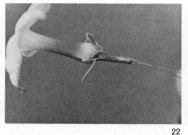

22

Mounting completed.

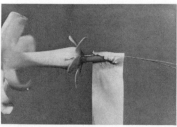

23

Commencement of guttaring.

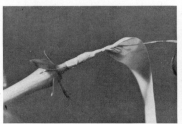

24

Halfway through guttaring.

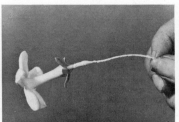

25

Mounting and guttaring completed.

26

Mounting a Chincherinchee floret
Insert a 32° × 7" Rose wire through the base of the floret.

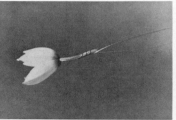

27

Halrpin Rose wire (4" and 3" legs) and wind 4" leg around the base of the stem.

28

Floret guttared.

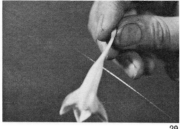

29

Point of insertion for a Freesia floret
Inserting a 32° × 7″ Rose wire.

30

Point of insertion for a Hyacinth Floret
Inserting a 32° × 7″ Rose wire.

Similar requirements for

Agapanthus	Hoya
Alstroemeria	Kaffir Lily
Clivia	Nerine
Crown Imperial	Rhododendron
Delphinium	Stock (double)
Gladioli (miniature)	Tuberose

Group D

Wiring a Lily of the Valley and mounting

31

Wiring
36° silver reel wire is wound from the bottom of the stalk upwards to the topmost floret to reinforce the stem and allow it to be bent as required.

32

Note that the reel wire is wound between *each* floret and a double twist is used around the top floret to finish.

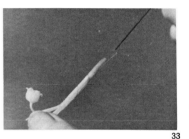

33

Mounting
Insert 22° × 14″ wire into the stem as far as possible (about ½″).

34

Wired Lily of the Valley mounted on wire.

35

Guttaring commenced.

36

Wiring, mounting and guttaring completed.

Group E

Wiring and mounting a Lily of theValley leaf

Wiring

Insert a 32° × 7″ Rose wire into the back of the leaf at the half way point allowing about ¼″ of it to project.

37

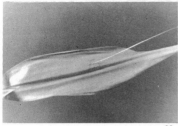

The ¼″ Rose wire projection is bent to form a loop.

38

The Rose wire is twisted around the stem of the leaf.

39

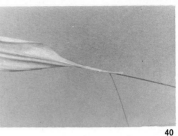

Mounting

A 22° × 14″ wire is inserted into the leaf stem and the Rose wire twisted around the wire to secure the mount in position.

40

Wiring and mounting completed.

41

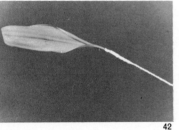

Guttaring completed.

42

Group F

Mounting a Gardenia

Similar requirements for Carnation, Dianthus, Gentian.

One Gardenia.

43

A 22° × 14″ wire is pushed into the calyx (not up the stem) and a 32° × 7″ Rose wire is threaded through the calyx horizontally to project 4″ on one side and 3″ on the other.

44

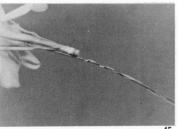

Both ends of the Rose wire have been bent to form a hairpin and brought parallel to the 14″ wire. The 4″ leg has been bound around the bottom of the Gardenia stem and also the 3″ leg and the 14″ wire. It is now ready for guttaring.

45

Group G

Wiring and mounting a single Rose leaf

Thread a 32° × 7″ Rose wire through the back of the Rose leaf at half way point

46

47

Rose wire is bent to form hairpin (4″ and 3″ legs) and the 4″ leg is wound around stem.

48

Wiring and mounting completed. Note that in addition to the leaf being mounted, the same wire has reinforced the actual leaf—constituting a wiring operation as well.

49

Guttared.
Similar requirements for
Gardenia leaf, Ivy leaf, Peperomia leaf, Pilea leaf, Rhododendron leaf, Tradescantia leaf.

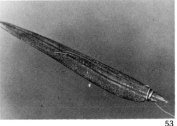

50

Leaf as pulled off stem.

51

Base of leaf trimmed with scissors to form a point.

52

32° × 7″ Rose wire "hooked" into the back of the leaf.

53

Wire taken down the leaf and wound around the trimmed base.

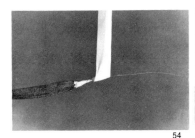

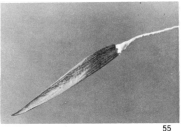

54

Guttaring.

55

Guttaring completed.

56

Take two mounted and guttared florets—see group C (stepped one below the other) and a 22° × 14″ wire.

57

Bind the three together with a 32°×7" Rose wire.

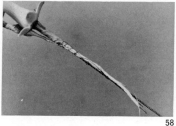
58

Mounting completed.

Note: One, two or even three florets or leaves which have been individually mounted on 32°×7" Rose wires can be mounted again on to 22°×14" wires,

59

Guttared.

thereby making them suitable for incorporation in all bouquets (other than sheaves).

60

Feathering a Carnation
The sepals of the Carnation are pulled back.

61

Three or more petals are removed.

62

Mounting a feathered Carnation
A 32°×7" Rose wire is pushed through the three petals and the two Rose wire projections (i.e. 3" and 4") are bent to form a hairpin. The 4" length is wound around the base of the petals.

63

Mounting completed. It may now be guttared and either one or two may be mounted on to a 22°×14"wire if required. (See 56 to 59.) *Note:* A group of individual petals from a Chrysanthemum bloom can be mounted similarly.

Group L

Mounting a feathered Carnation for a Victorian Posy

64

Mount a feathered Carnation (see 62 and 63). Insert a 24°×7" wire into the base of the wired petals.

65

Continue winding 4" length of Rose wire around the wire mount.

66

Gutta.

Group M

Mounting a Rose on a double leg for a Flower Ball

67

Insert a 24° × 7″ wire into the calyx.

68

Hairpin wire (4″ and 3″ legs).

69

4″ leg is wound around the stem and paralleled with the other leg. Rose now ready for insertion into flower ball—no guttaring required.

Group N

Wiring an Arum

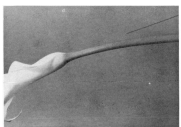

70

20° × 12″ wire being inserted into the stem.

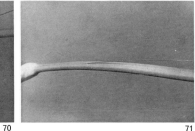

71

Wire having been inserted and pushed up about 3″ into the base of the flower head.

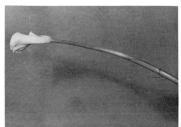

72

Wire twisted around the lower part of stem.

Group P

Mounting an Arum for an Arum Sheaf

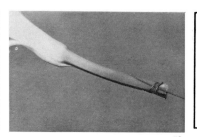

73

A shortened Arum cut to the required length mounted on to 20° × 12″ wire. (see 81, 82, 83 and 84)

Group Q

Wiring a Carnation for a Mixed Sheaf

Wiring various flowers for a Mixed Sheaf

74

Wiring a Carnation for a Mixed Sheaf
A 22° × 14″ wire being inserted into the base of the calyx.

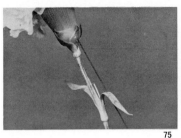

75

The wire has now been inserted.

76

The wire is wound around the Carnation stem.

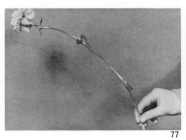

77

Wired Carnation ready for use—no guttaring required.

78

Wiring various flowers for a Mixed Sheaf

Point of insertion for the 22° × 14" wire when wiring an Iris for a Mixed Sheaf. Note that all foliage is removed.

79

Point of insertion for the 22° × 14" wire when wiring a Tulip for a Mixed Sheaf. Note that most of foliage is removed.

80

Point of insertion for the 22° × 14" wire when wiring a Rose for a Mixed Sheaf. Note *all* leaves removed.

Group R

Mounting a wired Carnation for a Mixed Sheaf Bouquet

81

Cutting the stem to the required length. (The longest mounted stem would be between $\frac{1}{3}$ and $\frac{1}{4}$ the *overall* length of the final bouquet and will govern the maximum dimensions of the "return end").

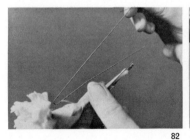

82

A 22° × 14" wire bent to a hairpin.

83

The hairpin wire has been placed against the bottom end of the Carnation stem and one leg of the hairpin is being wound around the stem and the other leg.

84

The hairpin leg which has been wound around the stem is being trimmed with scissors.

Assembly Techniques

INGREDIENTS

At the commencement of the instructional details of each design a list of the final ingredients will be found. An indication is also given of the Wiring and Mounting Group under which each ingredient has been prepared, the size of wire(s) used and "g" to indicate that guttaring (covering with Gutta-percha) is required, "ng" that it is not.

It will of course be appreciated that the ingredients which are used to assemble any particular design are very variable and the choice is dependent upon the colour scheme, size, bride's wishes, etc.

COLOUR

The colour scheme of the ingredients should be carefully selected, bearing in mind the bridal gown and the bridesmaids' dresses. The best way to develop a sense of colour is to study the work of experienced florists and to visit art galleries.

SIZE

It is important to bear in mind that bouquets should be carefully related to the size of the bride or bridesmaid. Small bouquets for small brides is an obvious but easily forgotten maxim.

SHAPE

The designs which are dealt with in the following Assembly section are basic ones and lend themselves to small variations. A graceful line is essential, and it is helpful to hold the bouquet in front of a mirror when it nears completion, to see that all is well in this respect before the handle is made and any alteration becomes impossible.

RETURN END

This term is used during the instructions for the assembly of certain bouquets. When approximately two-thirds of the bouquet has been completed, it becomes necessary to start inserting ingredients from the other end. When this stage is reached this part of the procedure is referred to as the "Return End" and, incidentally, establishes the overall length of the bouquet.

Assembly Techniques

Curved Shower Bouquet

85

Ingredients

10 double Freesias
  C & J 32° × 7″, 22° × 14″ g
1 single Freesia C & J 32° × 7″, 22° × 14″ g
5 double Stock C & J 32° × 7″, 22° × 14″ g
2 double tiny pink chiffon Rose buds
  C & J 32° × 7″, 22° × 14″ g
8 single pink chiffon Roses
  A 22° × 14″ g
11 single Lily of the Valley leaves
  E 32° × 7″, 22° × 14″ g
11 Lily of the Valley
  D 36° reelwire, 22° × 14″ g

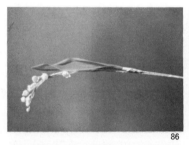

86

One Valley and one Valley leaf stepped and bound with 36° silver reel wire (two complete twists). (See 132.)

87

Another two flowers have been added and bound in.

88

Eight items now incorporated and bound together.

89

Sixteen items incorporated.
Note how bouquet is gradually taking shape and widening.

90

The seventeenth flower (i.e. a single Freesia) is being added. Note how the guttared wire is *twisted* around the other wires. As the bouquet becomes wider it is necessary for this twisting to be done every time a new item is added, otherwise

91

Twenty-five items. Front view.

the flowers tend to work out of their proper positions as the assembly progresses. The reel wire is, of course, still used to additionally secure the new ingredient.

92

Twenty-five items. Back view.

93

Thirty-five items. Maximum width has now been reached. Note the Rose is incorporated as a *centre* of interest.

94

Commencement of "return end." A Valley leaf is being incorporated to establish the *overall length* of the bouquet. Note how the wire is bent through approximately 180° before being twisted and bound into position.

95

Forty items. Note how the outline of the return end has now been added.

96

Fifty items. "Return end" now almost complete.

97

Completed bouquet from behind showing handle. (See 99-112.)

98

Curved Shower Bouquet.

99

Trimming and Ribboning a Handle
Bouquet wires before trimming.

100

Bouquet wires after trimming with scissors. The length of the handle depends upon the type of bouquet.

101

A 12″ × 1½″ strip of tissue paper being cut.

102

Tissue strip being placed on the handle.

103

Tissue being bound around the handle—similar to bandaging a finger.

104

Tissue paper being secured with "sello-tape".

105

Tissue paper binding completed.

106

2″ white satin ribbon being bound around the handle (exactly the same procedure as that used for tissue paper).

107

Ribbon binding continuing.

108

Ribbon binding completed. The ribbon has been cut and secured with two pins.

109

Making the bow

A length of ribbon (three times the eventual overall width of the bow) folded into three.

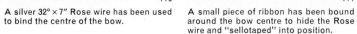

110

A silver 32° × 7″ Rose wire has been used to bind the centre of the bow.

111

A small piece of ribbon has been bound around the bow centre to hide the Rose wire and "sellotaped" into position.

112

The bow is pinned to the back of the handle.

Straight Shower Bouquet

113

Ingredients

11 double Freesias
      C & J 32° × 7″, 22° × 14″ g
11 Lily of the Valley
      D 36° reelwire, 22° × 14″ g
10 Lily of the Valley leaves
      E 32° × 7″, 22° × 14″ g
15 Roses   A 22° × 14″ g
3 double Rose leaves
      G & J 32° × 7″, 22° × 14″ g
2 single Rose leaves
      G & J 32° × 7″, 22° × 14″ g

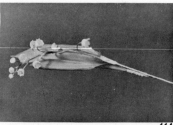

114

Leaf and Valley bound together with 36° silver reel wire.

115

Five items bound together.

116

Ten items bound together (front).

117

Ten items bound together (back).

118

Twenty items. Wire twisting is now starting as the maximum bouquet width is reached. (See 90.)

119

Close up of twisted wire.

120

Twenty-five items. Maximum width now reached.

121

Now is the stage to commence the "return end". Before this can be done it is necessary for the handle to be bent like a hairpin so that the bride can hold the *straight* Shower more naturally and with greater ease.

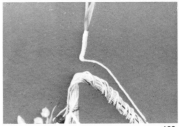

122

The first item of the "return end" (a leaf) being inserted to establish the overall length of the bouquet.

123

The "return end" leaf twisted and bound in position.

124

Bouquet with "return end" leaf—front view.

125

Thirty items. Two Valley and Two Freesia added to "return end".

126

Thirty items. Back view. Note handle.

127

Bouquet nearly completed. "Return end" outlined and filled in. Note open Rose as centre of interest.

128

Completed bouquet showing ribboned handle.

129

Straight Shower Bouquet.

Waterfall Bouquet

130

Ingredients

1 Orchid	A 22° × 14″ g
12 Daffodils	B 32° × 7″, 22° × 14″ g
9 Lily of the Valley leaves	
	E 32° × 7″, 22° × 14″ g
11 Lily of the Valley	
	D 36° reelwire, 22° × 14″ g
1 single Freesia	C & J 32° × 7″, 22° × 14″ g
7 double Freesias	
	C & J 32° × 7″ 22° × 14″ g

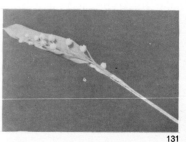

131

Two items. One Valley leaf and one Valley before being bound together.

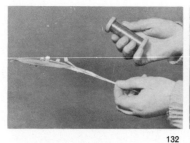

132

Two items at the commencement of the binding with 36° silver reel wire.

133

Four items. Note the left thumb holding a double Freesia in position before binding.

134

Six items from front view completing one of three trails.

135

Six items from behind.

136
Six items showing one trail in its entirety.

137
Eighteen items showing the three trails.

138
Two trails, the wires having been bent at a right angle, in position before binding. Note that one of these two trails is the *reversed* image of the other.

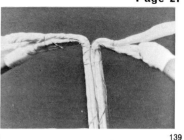
139
Close up of the binding together of the trails with 36° silver reel wire.

140
The third (centre) trail has now been incorporated.

141
Nineteen items. A central leaf has been added to give the overall height of the bouquet.

142
Twenty-six items. A further seven items have been added to fill in the rest of the outline.

143
Twenty-six items from behind.

144
Twenty-nine items. Note that the Orchid has been added as a centre of interest.

145
Final version with handle trimmed and ribboned, bow still to be added. Back view.

146
Waterfall Bouquet.

Orchid Bouquet

147
Ingredients

14 single leaves (Rhododendron)
G & J 32° × 7″, 22° × 14″ g
5 double leaves (Rhododendron)
G & J 32° × 7″, 22° × 14″ g
11 Cymbidium Orchids
A 22° × 14″ g

148
One double leaf and one Orchid stepped and bound together with 36° silver reel wire.

149
Ten items bound together (front view).

150
Ten items bound together (back view).

151
Fourteen items. Bouquet becoming wider so consequently the twisting of the wires of new ingredients around the handle now commences.

152
Fourteen items. Back view.

153
Twenty-two items. Note that all Orchids are now incorporated and the last one represents the "return end".

154
Twenty-two items (back view).

155
Final bouquet from behind before handle is trimmed.

156
Final bouquet from behind. Handle trimmed and ribboned.

157

Orchid Bouquet.

Rose Bouquet

Ingredients

24 Roses   A 22° × 14" g

9 double Rose leaves 6 single Rose leaves

G & J 32° × 7", 22° × 14" g

158

159

Rose and a double leaf, stepped and bound together with 36° silver reel wire.

160

Ten items bound together (front).

161

Ten Items (from behind).

162

Twenty items. Note that the width of the bouquet has now been established.

163

Close up of twenty items from behind. Note how binding wire has been, item by Item, gradually brought down to the point where the "return end" will have to be started.

164

Thirty items. Note the "return end" has already been commenced.

165

Thirty items from behind. Note that the wires are now being twisted around the handle.

166

Finished bouquet from behind with completed beribboned handle.

167

Rose Bouquet

Mixed Green Bouquet

Ingredients
163

3 Cyclamen leaves
G & J 32° × 7″, 22° × 14″ g
4 Canariensis leaves
G & J 32° × 7″, 22° × 14″ g
2 double and 3 single Pilea leaves
G & J 32°(7″, 22° × 14″ g
7 Berry clusters J 22° × 14″ g
(mounted direct on to 22° × 14″ wire)
5 Coleus leaves G & J 32° × 7″, 22° × 14″ g
(not recommended for lasting)
2 double Ivy leaves
G & J 32° × 7″, 22° × 14″ g
2 Tradescantia leaves
G & J 32° × 7″, 22° × 14″ g
11 Rhododendron leaves
G & J 32° × 7″, 22° × 14″ g
1 double Geranium leaf
G & J 32° × 7″, 22° × 14″ g

169
Two items. Rhododendron leaf with double Ivy leaves stepped and bound together.

170
Two items from behind.

171
Ten items.

172
Twenty items.

173
Twenty items from behind.

174
Thirty items.

175
Thirty items from behind.

176
Mixed Green Bouquet.

Crescent Bouquet

Ingredients

177

12 Lily of the Valley
D 36° reelwire, 22° × 14″ g
7 Daffodils
B 32° × 7″, 22° × 14″ g
1 Cymbidium
A 22° × 14″ g
8 Roses
A 22° × 14″ g
7 Cyclamen leaves
G & J 32° × 7″, 22° × 14″ g

178

One Valley with wire bent to form a right angle.

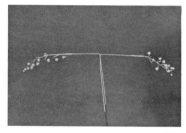

179

Two Valley with wires at right angles and bound together with 36° silver reel wire.

180

Three Valley (the third item upright). The outline of bouquet (width and height) has now been established.

181

Nine items. Outline now completed.

182

Nineteen items. Gradual filling in of the central part of bouquet. Note Orchid as centre of interest.

183

Nineteen items from behind.

184

Nineteen items. Close up of wire binding from behind.

185

Final version from behind with handle completed with ribbon.

186

Crescent Bouquet.

Posy Bouquet

Ingredients
187

12 Roses   A 22° × 14″ g
7 double Rose leaves
         G & J 32° × 7″, 22° × 14″ g
2 single Rose leaves
         G & J 32° × 7″, 22° × 14″ g
6 double Stephanotis
         C & J 32° × 7″, 22° × 14″ g
1 single Stephanotis
         C & J 32° × 7″, 22° × 14″ g
6 double Freesias
         C & J 32° × 7″, 22° × 14″ g
2 single Freesias
         C & J 32° × 7″, 22° × 14″ g

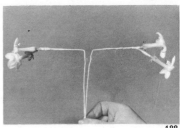

188
Two double Stephanotis at right angles.

189
First two items bound together with 36°
reel wire.

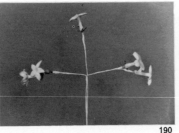

190
Three items bound together. Width and
height now established.

191
Seven items. Outline completed. It is
essential that all the items should have
the same radius so that a circular bouquet
results.

192
Close up of the seven-item outline bound
together.

193
A double Rose leaf bent ready for incorporation into the lower half of bouquet.

194
Double Rose leaf being placed in position
prior to being bound in.

195
Double Rose leaf bound in.

196
Fifteen items. Note that double Rose leaf
referred to in 193, 194, 195 has now been
bent slightly to take up a position to the
right of the handle. Filling in has now
commenced.

197

Fifteen items from behind.

198

Twenty items from the front.

199

Twenty-eight items. Bouquet nearly completed.

200

Completed bouquet from behind with beribboned handle.

201

Posy Bouquet.

Mixed
Sheaf
Bouquet

202

Ingredients

6 Iris	Q 22° × 14″ ng
7 Carnations	Q 22° × 14″ ng
9 Tulips	Q 22° × 14″ ng
8 Roses	Q 22° × 14″ ng

All items are *wired* with 22° × 14″ wires on their natural stems. The items used in the "return end" are also mounted. (see Group R.)

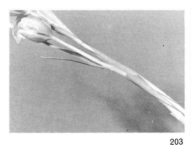

203

Two items. One Iris and one Tulip being bound together with 32° silver reel wire.

204

Ten items from the front view.

205

Ten items from behind. Note how the reel wire binding has gradually travelled downwards.

206

Fifteen items. The widest point of bouquet has now been reached and the reel wire is finished off at this stage before the "return end" is commenced.

207

Close up of the end of the reel wire before being pushed home into the stems to secure.

208

Eighteen items. Two *mounted* flowers (Rose and Iris) have been incorporated into the "return end". The third flower (a *mounted* Carnation) is now being inserted. (See group R for mounting.)

209

Close-up. The wire of the mounted "return end" flower has been pushed right through the stems and then twisted around the stalks — the end then being bent and pushed home into the stalks.

210

Twenty-five items. When the final bouquet is completed, the wires remaining on the natural stems of the flowers which were incorporated *before* the "return end" was commenced are unwound up to the twisted mounts and cut off.

211

Back view. Close up of wiring and mounts before ribboning.

212

Close up of ribbon which has been used to cover mounts. Note how the stems at the end of the bouquet have been trimmed and graduated.

213

Final version from behind.

214

Mixed Sheaf Bouquet.

Arum Sheaf

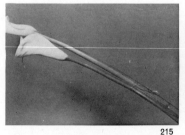

215

Ingredients
12 Arum Lilies   N 20° × 12" ng
    five of which P mounted on 20° × 12"
Two wired Arums (see 70, 71, 72) stepped and bound together with 32° silver reel wire.

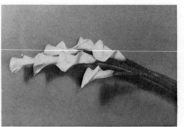

216

Seven wired Arums bound together. Note careful spacing. There are comparatively few blooms and each one shows up conspicuously. No more Arums will be bound in. Remaining five will be "mounted". (See 73.)

217

The binding wire has been cut off from the reel and the end is being inserted into a nearby fleshy stem.

218

The reel wire end has been pushed home.

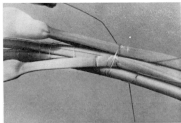

219

The wire of the *mounted* Arum pushed through the fleshy stems at the point where the binding wire was finished off.

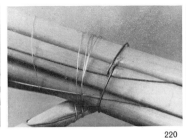

220

The mounting wire has now been wound around the stems and the end pushed into one of the stalks.

221

Eight Arums. The mounted Arum is now in position (top right).

222

All twelve Arums now incorporated (last five have all been *mounted* and inserted as shown.)

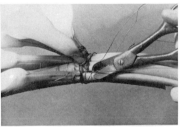

223

The wires which were used to wire the first seven Arums are now unwound from their natural stems as far as the point where the mounts have been wound around the stalks. They are then cut off with scissors.

224

Close up of wiring and mounts.

225

A ribbon has been bound around to hide the mounts, and a bow added.

226

Arum Sheaf. Note the bottom of the stems have been trimmed slantwise and, at the same time, slightly graduated.

Prayer Book Spray

(right angled)

227

Ingredients

1 Rose	A 24° × 7″ g
7 Rose leaves	G 32° × 7″ g
9 feathered Carnations	K 32° × 7″ g
7 Freesias	C 32° × 7″ g
14 Freesia buds (single and double)	C 32° × 7″ g

228

One leaf and one Freesia bud stepped and bound together with 36° silver reel wire.

229

Seventeen items. Assembled in similar fashion to a mixed corsage. (See 377-383).

230

Seventeen items. At this stage the handle is bent to form a right angle.

231

Eighteen items. One Freesia has now been bound to the bent handle.

232

Twenty-three items. Working back along the handle. The Rose has been incorporated to form a focal point (when in position it will be on top of the prayer book).

233

Twenty-four items. One leaf has just been incorporated to start a small "return end". It is bound in and *then* bent back into its correct position.

234

Final version with "return end" completed.

235

The 1½" satin ribbon is inserted at the "marriage service". Its length is approximately 18" plus twice the length of the prayer book.

236

One end of the ribbon has been brought over the prayer book cover and stitched to allow a double tail of about 9".

237

The prayer book spray is placed in position and secured either with "sellotape" (in the case of a lightweight small spray) or stitched.

238

Right-angled Prayer Book Spray. Note how the ends of the ribbon are trimmed and stepped.

Prayer Book Spray
(straight)

Ingredients

239

4 feathered Carnations	K 32° × 7″ g
5 Freesias	C 32° × 7″ g
9 Freesia buds	C 32° × 7″ g
7 Rose leaves	G 32° × 7″ g

The ingredients have been assembled in a similar fashion to the method outlined for making a mixed corsage (see 377-383).

240

One end of the 1½″ satin ribbon is taken through the "marriage service", the other under the back cover. They are then stitched together giving a tail of approximately 9″, to which the spray is secured by stitching or "sellotaping".

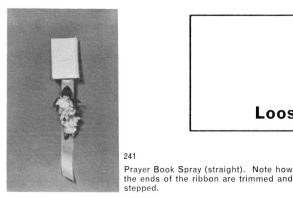

241

Prayer Book Spray (straight). Note how the ends of the ribbon are trimmed and stepped.

Loose Posy

Ingredients

242

5 Daffodils	B 32° × 7″, 22° × 14″ g
6 Roses	A 22° × 14″ g
11 double Freesias	C & J 32° × 7″, 22° × 14″ g
1 single Freesia	C & J 32° × 7″, 22° × 14″ g
7 Rose leaves	G & J 32° × 7″, 22° × 14″ g
4 Cyclamen leaves	G & J 32° × 7″, 22° × 14″ g

243

One double Freesia with wire bent to form a right angle.

244

Two double Freesias with right-angled wires bound together with 36° silver reel wire.

245

The outline of five right-angled double Freesias.

246

The outline of five double Freesias from another viewpoint.

247

Six items. The Rose has been incorporated upright to establish the height of the posy—about the same as the radius.

248

Eighteen items. Note how the outline has been filled in.

249

Final posy before the handle has been trimmed.

250

Final posy with trimmed and ribboned handle.

251

Loose posy.

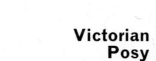

Victorian Posy

252

Ingredients

17 feathered Carnations
    K & L 32° × 7″, 24° × 7″ g
9 Chrysanthemum florets   B 24° × 7″ g
9 Freesias   C & J 32° × 7″, 24° × 7″ g
7 Carole Roses   A 24° × 7″ g
1 frill

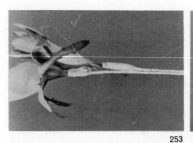

253

A Rose and a Freesia bound together with 36° silver reel wire.

254

Seven items. Notice how the central Rose is raised above the other ingredients.

255

Thirteen items. Seven Roses have now been incorporated.

256

Close-up of binding. Note how perimeter flowers are bent slightly to position them.

257

Twenty-two items. A circle of Chrysanthemum florets have now been added.

258

Thirty-nine items looking from underneath. Feathered Carnations have now been incorporated.

259

The handle wires of the final version—before trimming.

260

The silver reel wire has been bound around the handle wires right down to the bottom—bringing the wires closely together.

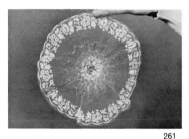
261

The frill.

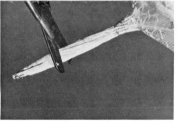
262

The handle being shortened to about 6". Note that the frill has been put in position —it may be necessary to enlarge the central frill hole slightly by slitting. (see cardboard mount for Gardenia, 391-4) but the frill should fit close to the handle.

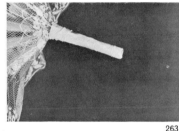
263

The handle has been guttared. There is no need to use tissue paper as the handle, not having been "twisted", is already thin and neat.

264

The handle has been ribboned.

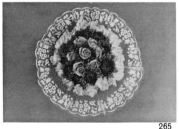
265

Victorian Posy.

Flower Ball

266

Ingredients

Moss
Ribbon for handle

12 Chrysanthemum florets	M 24° × 7″ ng
13 Freesias	M 24° × 7″ ng
18 Carole Roses	M 24° × 7″ ng
14 feathered Carnations	M 24° × 7″ ng

Each flower is mounted on to a 24° × 7″ wire (see 67, 68, 69) and the length of each mount is cut down to slightly less than the diameter of the moss ball.

267

Moss ball being prepared. A handful of sphagnum moss is bound with 32° silver reel wire into a ball shape. The reel wire is taken around the ball, in various directions, about ten times in order to keep the shape.

268

Mounting a ribbon for the handle. About 12″ of 1″ satin ribbon is doubled and the two free ends are mounted on a 22° × 14″ wire.

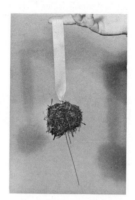

269

The double wire of the ribbon mount is pushed through the moss ball, trimmed so that about 1″ projects, and the projections are bent back and pushed home into the moss.

270

The handle has been inserted first so that the ball can be hung whilst flowers are inserted into position. A mounted Rose is about to be inserted into the moss ball.

271

Rose has been inserted and pushed home.

272

Eight items have now been inserted.

273

Nearly all the flowers are now inserted. Note small amount of moss still visible and requiring further items to cover.

274

All the flowers have been inserted and the moss should now be completely covered. •

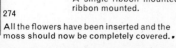

275

A single ribbon mounted and a double ribbon mounted.

276

A Flower Ball. Three single mounted ribbons and three double ones have been inserted around the handle, to finish.

Bridesmaid's Basket

Ingredients

277

7 Rose leaves	G & J
10 Chrysanthemum florets	B & J
15 Carole Roses	A & J
10 Freesias	C & J

All items are initially mounted on a 24° × 7" wire and guttared. Later they are mounted on to another 24° × 7" wire. (see 281)

Basket.

278

Sphagnum moss to be used in basket.

279

Moss put into basket.

280

Mounted item mounted again on to a 24° × 7" wire ready for insertion into moss.

281

Fourteen items inserted to provide outline, including the central flower which governs the height of the arrangement.

282

Fourteen items from above.

283

Nineteen items. Note that the outline is now being filled in.

284

Final version from above.

285

Bridesmaid's Basket.

286

Cluster Headdress

287

Ingredients

4 feathered Carnations   K
10 Freesias   C
2 Rose buds   C
2 Chrysanthemum florets   C
18 Rose leaves   G

All items mounted on 32° × 7″ Rose wires.
All except 8 Rose leaves are guttared.

288

One Freesia and one Rose bud stepped and bound together.

289

Five items bound together.

290

Ten items.

291

Fifteen items from behind.

292

Fifteen items from the front. This is one of the two clusters required. Note how the leaves at the base have been bent back so as to cover the handle.

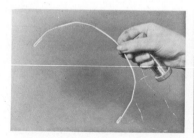

293

Headdress frame. Note the reel wire has been bound around one end of the frame in preparation for the attachment of one of the twin clusters. (See 315, 316 for frame construction.)

294

Cluster bound to the frame with 36° silver reel wire.

295

Second cluster has now been bound to the frame.

296

A leaf mounted as usual on 32° × 7″ Rose wire, but not guttared, is being secured so as to cover the remaining central section of frame. (See 303, 304.)

297

Several more "covering" leaves attached to frame.

298

Cluster Headdress.

Alice Band
Headdress

299

Ingredients

4 Freesias	C
10 Rose leaves	G
5 Chrysanthemum buds	C
8 feathered Carnations	K
2 Freesia buds	C

All items mounted on 32° × 7" Rose wires. No guttaring.

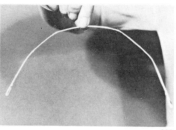

300

Frame with loops at both ends. The dimensions of the frame are dependent upon the size of head. The looped ends should be just above the ears.

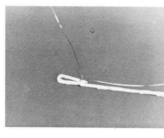

301

One of the looped ends being bound with 36° silver reel wire.

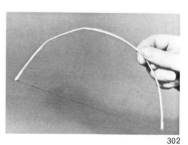

302

A length of hat elastic is tied to each loop of the frame.

303

A leaf being placed in position.

304

One of the legs being used to secure the leaf by binding it to the frame.

305

Three items bound with their own legs on to the frame. It is necessary to trim away some of each leg as the assembly progresses.

306

Three items from behind.

307

Eleven items. This is the completion of the first half. Note how the last wire leg has been trimmed and finished off by binding neatly around the frame.

308

Eleven items from the side view.

309

Thirteen items. Two items have been attached to the other end of the frame.

310

Twenty-three items. Both sides of the frame have been completed and a Chrysanthemum has been inserted in the central portion as a centre of interest.

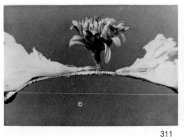

311

A close-up showing central Chrysanthemum.

312

Completed headdress. Note how flowers have been incorporated on either side of centre of interest (i.e. Chrysanthemum).

313

Alice Band Headdress.

Rose Backspray Headdress

314

Ingredients

5 Carole Roses   A
16 Rose leaves   G

Roses mounted on 24° × 7″ wires and guttared. Rose leaves mounted on 32° × 7″ wires and guttared.

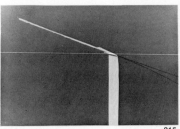

315

Making frame. Two 22° × 14″ wires (reduce wire length for tiny child) are placed together and guttared tightly.

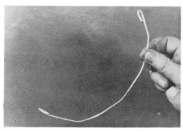

316

The frame is bent to form a semi-circle and the two ends are bent back to form loops.

317

One leaf is bound with 36° silver reel wire to one end of the frame.

318

Two leaves. The second leaf overlaps the first one and is bound to the frame.

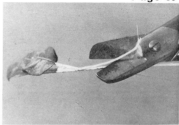

319

The projecting guttered wire of the second leaf is removed with scissors.

320

Note the small remaining stub after removal of surplus with scissors.

321

Note stub has now been bound to frame with reel wire.

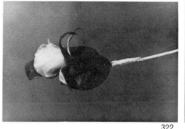

322

Five items. Note how surplus wire has been removed after each item is bound in.

323

Five items from back view.

324

Eleven items from the front.

325

Eleven items from behind. This is the halfway stage and the 36° silver reel wire is ended off, before further items are bound in from the other end of the frame.

326

One leaf bound to the other end of the frame (obscuring loop).

327

Seventeen items. Headdress is nearly complete. A few more leaves required to fill in around the central Rose.

328

Completed headdress—back view.

329

Rose Backspray Headdress.

Mixed Backspray Headdress

330

Ingredients

6 Freesias, C. 4 feathered Carnations, K. 1 Rose, C. 4 tiny Rose buds, C. 11 Rose leaves, G. All items are mounted on 32° × 7" wires and guttared.

331

The frame is the same as that used for the Rose Backspray Headdress. One leaf has been bound to one end of the frame.

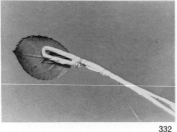

332

One leaf in position (back view).

333

Seven items. Note that the unnecessary guttared wires of each item have been trimmed away with scissors.

334

Fouteen items. The halfway stage has now been reached.

335

Fourteen items. Back view.

336

Fifteen items. One leaf has been bound to the other end of the frame.

337

Twenty-one items. Gradually working towards the centre.

338

Mixed Backspray Headdress.

Circlet Headdress

339

Ingredients

10 feathered Carnations	K
8 Kaffir Lily florets	C
10 Chincherinchee florets	C
9 small Ivy leaves	G

All mounted on 32° × 7″ wires. n.g.

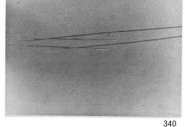

340

Making frame. Four 22° × 14″ wires about to be joined.

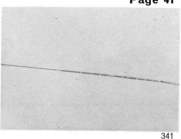

341

The double wires have been joined and bound together with 36° silver reel wire to make a total length of about 24″ (i.e. 28″ less the 4″ central join).

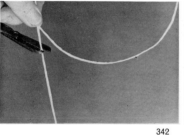

342

After the frame has been guttared, it is bent into a complete circle. (The diameter is dependent upon the wearer's head) and any surplus frame wire is removed with scissors.

343

The two ends of the frame are each looped. One loop is bound with 36° silver reel wire and the other loop is hooked into it.

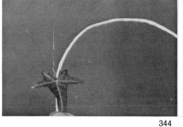

344

One leaf being placed in position. Note double wire leg.

345

The leaf is being secured by binding one of the legs around the other which lies along the frame.

346

Two items bound to the frame.

347

The surplus wires (after securing) being removed with scissors.

348

Four items incorporated.

349

Ten items.

350

Ten items from behind.

351

Twenty items. Note how full circle is gradually being covered.

352

Thirty items.

353

Circlet Headdress.

Chignon Headdress

354

Ingredients
6 feathered Carnations   K
8 Rose leaves G   2 Stephanotis C
4 Freesia C   1 Rose C
All items mounted on to 32° × 7″ wires. No guttaring.

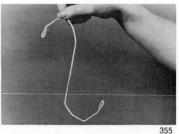

355

"S" type frame. Two 22° × 14″ wires have been bound together, guttared, shaped to an "S" and the two ends looped.

356

One leaf (with double wire leg) bound to one end of the frame in a similar fashion to the circlet headdress. (See 345.)

357

Six items have been bound to the frame and surplus wires trimmed away.

358

Six items from behind.

359

Eight items. Seven items have been bound to one end of the frame and one leaf to other—commencing the return.

Thirteen items. Six items have now been incorporated into the "return end".

360

361

Thirteen items from behind.

362

Final version from behind.

363

Chignon Headdress.

Rose Corsage

Ingredients (not illustrated)

3 Roses   A

7 Rose leaves   G

Roses are mounted on 22° × 14″ wires and guttared.

Rose leaves are mounted on 32° × 7″ Rose wires and guttared.

364

One Rose and one leaf, stepped and bound together with 36° silver reel wire.

365

One Rose and two leaves.

366

One Rose and three leaves from behind.

367

Two Roses and three leaves incorporated.

368

Three Roses and five leaves bound together. Note that by *not* putting the Roses in a straight line, character is imparted to the corsage.

369

Three Roses and seven leaves. Note how lower two leaves are bent back to cover wires and to give corsage shape.

370

Final version from behind. Note that handle has been trimmed and guttared and a pin inserted for wearer's use.

371

Rose Corsage.

Orchid Corsage

Ingredients (not illustrated)

2 Cymbidiums   A

9 small Rhododendron leaves   G

Orchids mounted on 22° × 14″ wire and guttared. Leaves mounted on 32° × 7″ wire and guttared.

372

First two items bound together with 36° silver reel wire.

373

One Orchid and three leaves bound together.

374

Two Orchids and three leaves.

375

Two Orchids and nine leaves from behind, before handle has been trimmed and guttared.

376

Orchid Corsage.

Mixed Corsage

Ingredients (not illustrated)

5 Chincherinchee florets   C

3 Chincherinchee tips   C

4 Freesias   C

2 Rose leaves   G

2 Ivy leaves   G

5 Tradescantia leaves   G

6 Lilliput Zinnias   B

Zinnias are mounted on a 24° × 7″ wire and guttared. The remaining items are mounted on 32° × 7″ wires and guttared.

377

1 Chincherinchee tip and 1 Tradescantia leaf being bound together with 36° silver reel wire.

378

Five items bound together.

379

Eight items from behind.

380

Thirteen items.

381

Twenty items. Note how the last two items have been bent slightly to give maximum width to corsage.

382

Final version from behind. The short handle has been trimmed and guttared and a pin inserted for wearer's use.

383

Mixed Corsage.

Carnation Corsage

Ingredients (not illustrated)

9 Carnation leaves	H
2 Carnations	F

Leaves are mounted on 32° × 7" wires and guttared. Carnations are mounted on 22° × 14" wires and guttared.

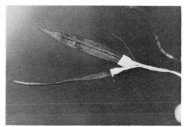

384

Two leaves being bound together with 36° silver reel wire.

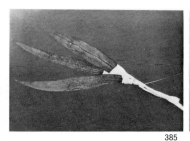

385

Three leaves bound together.

386

Four items. The first Carnation has now been incorporated.

387

Five items from behind.

388

Nine items from behind.

389

Final version from behind. Note handle has been trimmed and guttared and a pin inserted for wearer's use.

390

Carnation Corsage.

Gardenia Buttonhole

Ingredients (not illustrated)

5 Gardenia leaves   G
1 Gardenia   F

Leaves are mounted on 32° × 7″ wires and guttared. Gardenia is mounted on a 24° × 7″ wire and guttared.

391

A 1″ disc of white postcard being cut, using a coin.

392

The disc folded in half and having a small cut made centrally.

393

The disc folded the other way and a second cut being made at right angles to the first cut.

394

The completed disc.

395

The disc slipped over the Gardenia calyx to the base of the petals, in order to stop petals drooping.

396

One leaf has been bound to the Gardenia with 36° silver reel wire.

397

Final version from behind before the small handle has been trimmed and guttared.

398

Gardenia Buttonhole.

Wedding Cake Decoration

339

Ingredients

7 feathered Carnations	K & J
9 Lily of the Valley	D & J
9 Rose leaves	G & J
10 single Freesias	C & J
3 double Freesias	C & J
3 Freesia buds	C & J

All items are mounted on to 32° × 7″ wires except Lily of the Valley which is wired with 36° reel wire. They are then all mounted again on to 24° × 7″ wires and guttared.

400

Wineglass filled with "oasis".

401

Eight items inserted into "oasis" to create an outline.

402

Nine items. One Valley has been added to govern the overall height.

403

Final version looking like a miniature flower arrangement.

404

Wedding Cake Decoration.